MINDFUL WISDOM

From My

PHILOSOPHER DAD

Sage Advice from a Single Father

Tanya MacIntyre

Stay Positive, Chris!

♡ Tanya

Mindful Wisdom From My PHILOSOPHER DAD

Copyright 2018 Tanya MacIntyre

ISBN: 978-1-988215-39-6

All rights reserved.

While the principles and practices of Mindfulness and the Law of Attraction and other techniques discussed in this book are simple to use - and have produced remarkable results for some people - they must be used at your own risk. The author cannot and does not guarantee any specific results, and reminds the reader to take responsibility for their own use of these techniques.

Tanya MacIntyre can be reached at:
Email: tanya@gottalovelove.com

Website: www.PhilosopherDad.com

Layout by One Thousand Trees
Printed in Canada by M&T Printing Group

TABLE OF CONTENTS

ACKNOWLEDGEMENTS

I would like to express my gratitude to the countless people who helped me through the process of getting this book finished and published. It was a joint effort, to say the least, and I thank you!

To my clan of friends, colleagues, and supporters who kept encouraging me to move forward and keep making progress in this tribute to my father, my mentor, my best friend, my Philosopher Dad.

They are: Lance Lickfold, Chantal McIntyre, Terry Hallman, Liz Lermitte, Lee Pryke, Lisa Dadd, Renate Donnovan, Chris Patton, Russell Scott, Sheryl Plouffe, Dana Smithers, Peter Wright, Teresa Syms, Craig Dubecki, Lisa Browning, my followers and supporters online, and the people who keep coming to my events, THANK YOU.

DEDICATION

To my sister, Chantal, without whom I would be an only, lonely child who never had the gift of a baby sister who lights my path and guides my life choices to always strive to be a good example and the best version of myself.

To my nephew, Tyler, who constantly teaches me the true meaning of life... to live in the NOW, and love every precious, juicy, morsel of life.

To my husband, Lance, who was – on paper – my Prince Charming... and who is – in reality – my King who rules my world as a golden, sparkling treasure that keeps me healthy, wealthy, sexy, grateful, and joyous.

To my dad, Connie (short for Connington), who stepped up to the plate to be a single father in the 60s and raised his 2 little girls to be two of the most independent, head-strong, opinionated people on earth, who are also among the most loving, generous, heart-based population that aligns with all that's good in the world.

LETTER TO DAD
WHILE TRYING TO FINISH THIS BOOK

January 19, 2017

Dear Dad,

I've been struggling to finish this book for over 10 years, and I feel defeated and hopeless even thinking about it. I wanted to finish it while you were still alive – to read it and celebrate it with me – but that was not to be.

I thought grieving your death would get easier with each passing year, but it isn't getting easier at all.

I've read countless books on "the grief process," and have been through cognitive therapy and grief counseling.... but, I still have sobbing cries when I think of how much I miss you in my life! They say crying is therapeutic, so why the hell does it still hurt so much!?

Every time I try to finish this book I become too emotional and decide to wait another day. The day turns into a week, which turns into a month, and another month...and then another year has passed. I keep procrastinating, so I can keep avoiding the feelings of discomfort and the deep sadness of my grief.

I remember how you used to always encourage me to learn something new every day, even if it was just a new word.

I remember how I used to wait for you to get home every

night so we could talk about our days and about what I'd learned, and how much I wanted to hear what you thought about what I learned because I knew I'd always learn more from our conversations! I miss that so much, Dad. I miss having you in my life. I miss your mentorship and your friendship, and your tireless encouragement and support in my life.

As the years pass, and my grief lingers, I begin to realize that this grief will stay with me forever… but – as long as I keep working on peace and balance in my life - the grief becomes a bit lighter and I learn to carry it differently.

Thanks for your mindful wisdom throughout my life, Dad. I was so lucky to have you as a guide in this journey. I just wish you could be here to kick me in the ass right now to get me going to finish the damn book!

The Mills of the Gods Grind Slowly, but Exceedingly Fine.

I grew up hearing that quote SEVERAL TIMES from my Philosopher Dad.

I can still remember the first time I heard it, when I was about 9 years old. I had been bullied at school and came home in tears to ask my dad – between sobs – "Why are those girls being so mean to me, Daddy?"

He hugged me and said, "Don't worry sweetheart; the mills of the Gods grind slowly, but exceedingly fine."

The sentiment was lost on me as a 9-year-old, but it was a line of philosophy that has stayed with me throughout my life.

A more popular version of the quote is, basically, "What goes around comes around."

That was the foundation set for me by my Philosopher Dad during my childhood. I grew up believing that we reap what we sow, *so it's really important to plant good seeds.*

So, having had that "good" foundation in life, it's ironic that I ended up in a career in mainstream media — which is an industry that does anything but plant good seeds.

I spent 22 years as a broadcast journalist, before I finally came to the realization that the purpose of mainstream media is to perpetuate fear, uncertainty, and doubt (the FUD Factor). There's a saying in the media ranks — "If it bleeds, it leads." Sad, but true. The more sensational the story the better.

My first awakening came when I was one of the first Toronto reporters on the scene of the Swiss Air crash at Peggy's Cove in 1998. It was a feeding frenzy of media unlike anything I had ever experienced. I spent the day doing live reports of the carnage and despair, and the ongoing speculation of how the crash happened... and then I had what I can only describe as a mental meltdown.

I decided that I needed to switch gears and highlight a positive aspect of this devastating event. I had spoken to residents in and around the area who were prepared to open their hearts and homes to the family members who would be arriving shortly from overseas to grieve over what little remained of their loved ones.

The collective voice was resounding: that it was important for these families to be greeted with love and compassion.

Nobody wanted to see these people standing at a hotel desk to check into a bleak, empty room in a strange city. That became my story.

When I filed the first report, my news director came on the line afterwards and said "What the fu** is this crap!? I want to see the blood and feel the pain!!!"

I remember standing there, in the phone booth (yes, phone booth. It was only 1998, remember, so cell phones were still rare and very expensive). So, I was standing inside the phone booth in downtown Halifax, holding the phone away from my ear, looking at the phone in disbelief, and thinking to myself "I can't do this anymore."

I ended up staying in that vocation for another 5 years, though. It was a career that had defined my entire adult life at that time, so it scared me to even think of leaving it. What would I do? Who would I be?!

I ended up working at a heritage radio station in small-town Ontario — as news director. The station's motto was, "Where Local News Comes First!" I thought, "This could be good for me. I was from a small town, and I've returned to a small town!" It was an OK salary, it came with a rare 4-week vacation, and it was close to home. I thought I had landed my dream job!

But, that all changed in 2003 when the US and allied forces invaded Iraq.

On the day of "shock and awe," I led my first newscast with a story about our local Red Cross and the work they were doing on a humanitarian level. My boss called me after my first broadcast to ask me, "Where is our war coverage?" I told him that this was an unsanctioned war that should see George Bush charged with treason, and that I was not prepared to perpetuate the American propaganda.

That day marked the end of my illustrious broadcasting career.

I have dedicated my life to positive media ever since, and founded **The Good News Only** in 2010. I am finally planting some good seeds!

WHY I WROTE THIS BOOK

My dad became a single parent of me and my little sister in 1969, so that would have made him 39.

Our mother was a chronic and hopeless alcoholic who ran away with a Navy Captain when his ship came to port in our little coal-mining town.

I was 9, my sister was 2.

There were not many single fathers around in 1969, and there wasn't a parenting handbook for him to follow (other than Dr. Spock, whose advice I'm sure he may have referred to at times).... so my dad really had to wing it on his own.

Thankfully, he was an avid reader, and he used to quote people from his readings ALL the time.

He would routinely offer a line of philosophy to me or my sister, whenever we went to him with a problem.

I grew to lovingly and jokingly call him "Philosopher Dad."

This is my tribute to him.

Everything Happens for a Reason.

I stood on the lawn of my aunt's house, anxiously awaiting the return of my dad. It was his day in court; the day a judge would decide where my sister and I would live. The custody battle was long and bitter, and – in 1970 – the chances were remote that my dad would be awarded custody.

But, I thought... how could a judge not see that we were better off living with our dad? We had been with him for almost a year, after he successfully won temporary custody that was ordered by children's services after a home visit found no food in the fridge or cupboards, and no sign of our mother.

Dad's car pulled into the driveway, as my heart pounded with anticipation and my stomach churned with fear. I could tell by his posture that the news was not good.

We had to go back and live with our mother!

Things didn't improve with Mom. Her drinking escalated, as did her escapades. The men came and went, as did our babysitters.

My mother was a chronic alcoholic (I know first-hand that there are several different levels of alcoholism). She grew up a coal miner's daughter in a little town that loves to gossip. She married my father when she was 21 and still a virgin. Dad was 30, so maybe she saw him as the ideal father figure. She didn't like her own father very much, and spent her life blaming him for pretty much everything.

The straw that broke the proverbial camel's back was the

day I came home from school to hear my baby sister's cries from our apartment. I ran in to find her frightened little body stuck on the toilet. Our babysitter had sat her on the toilet, where she lost her balance and fell into the toilet... unable to lift her tiny bum out of the hole! To add insult to injury, the babysitter thought it would be funny to turn out the bathroom light and close the door, while Chantal screamed and cried in terror. She was not much older than 3 at the time, and it took many years for her to sleep in a dark room, and even longer for her to sleep in a dark room with the door closed.

That's when Dad decided the best course of action was to play my mother's money game. He bribed her to sign over full custody. He would never disclose the amount it took for her to sign away her custody privileges, but I never asked more than once.

The next several years were filled with a loving and hard-working father who struggled as a single parent, but embraced the challenge with love and lots of positivity, humour, and insight. He had no idea how to be a parent, but he did his best to raise his two little girls with all he could provide.

As a child, I would definitely not have wanted to hear someone say "Everything happens for a reason," but as an adult I can now appreciate that everything comes into our life for a reason (which is normally to teach us a lesson, push us beyond our comfort zone, and/or motivate us to change).

It's not WHAT happens in our life that's key to our life balance and peace of mind, it's HOW we deal with what happens in our life.

One of my favourite interviews was with psychologist Sean Stephenson, who is known as the 3-foot giant. Sean has osteogenesis imperfecta, and has suffered much pain in his life. When he was about 5-6 years old, he broke his femur while getting ready to go out for Halloween. While he rolled around in excruciating pain, his mother said to him, "Sean, you can consider your life and this reality a burden or a blessing... you decide." Sean says that one sentence put him on a path of gratitude and self-empowerment.

Journal entry October 11, 2015 – edited for clarity

I just finished another cry, a sobbing cry... a cry that takes all my energy by the mere virtue of shedding the emotion associated with the tears... that feeling that starts at the pit of my stomach and seeps up to my heart and stings like a stabbing pain.

I've had so many of those sobbing cries that, by the time my father was ravaged and finally taken by a hideous and merciless disease, the cries had taken a toll. When Dad died in 2010, it was almost a relief.

He had been diagnosed with Alzheimer's in 2005. In the early stages of the disease, he was very bitter and angry... especially after failing the requisite driver's test and having his license revoked. It was just the beginning of a very unpleasant journey.

I've lost my father, my friend, my mentor, my hero.... the man who made me the woman I've become. He brought me up as a single father, along with my younger sister – who in many ways is more like a daughter to me.

After our mother left us, Dad was working 14+-hour days in real estate sales and service; something he really didn't enjoy doing but it was something that provided us with a certain lifestyle...a lifestyle he felt we deserved — perhaps as compensation for being abandoned by our mother.

And then, after the diagnosis, I finally had what I had longed to have while I was growing up... my father's undivided time and attention. Oh how I had longed for that luxury when I was in my pre-teen and teen years.

If there is a positive aspect of Alzheimer's, it is that the diagnosis gave us the time to appreciate what little time we had left with each other.

In all the years I lived and worked with my Dad, I never heard him say anything negative about anyone.

He instilled a moral foundation in me and my sister by his daily example.

My relationship with my father has undoubtedly made me the person I am, the person who is sometimes too direct, too abrupt, too cynical... and far too impatient and undiplomatic.

I have, ironically, become everything my father wasn't. How does that happen?!

Aging Ain't for Sissies

In 2007, just before I left Canada for Spain, Dad and I spent a week together in the Dominican Republic. In the 2 years since his diagnosis, he had adapted fairly well to the changes.

He accepted the loss of independence, to a degree. After he lost his driver's license, he purchased a motorized bicycle. He only drove it a few months before his sense of balance failed him one day while riding on a busy road. He called me, sounding panicked. He had lost his balance and driven into a ditch. He wasn't hurt... just very shaken. Thankfully, my husband – Lance – was home that day and drove to where Dad was to pick up him and the bike. Dad never drove the bike again. Lance later told me that when he pulled over to the side of the road that day Dad was sitting in the ditch and looked like a lost and frightened little boy.

When Dad and I decided to take a vacation together, we needed to book a double room because he needed assistance to dress himself, and his balance was so bad he was at risk of falling all the time. Mentally, he was still sharp... but physically he was failing fast.

It was a bit of a challenge for us to share a room together. One morning, while Dad was showering, I sat on the patio to soak up some sun and read. After a few minutes, I heard the shuffling of feet behind me, and Dad's voice saying "I need your help with my underwear. I think I have them on backwards because I can't find the crotch." When I turned around and looked, I said, "Dad, you can't find the crotch because you're wearing MY underwear."

That was among the many laughs we shared during that week, many of which involved him trying to put on my clothes.

At least – I told myself – he was not in any physical pain... the pain for him was mental... to realize what was happening to him, to be losing his mind, and struggling to accept the reality of what that meant.

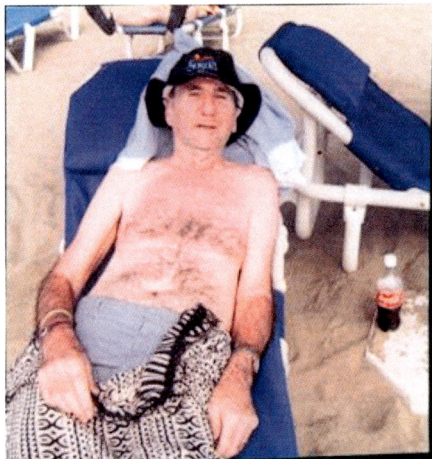

Dad on vacation, 2005

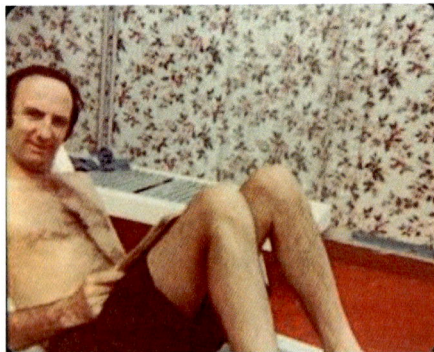

Dad on vacation, 1975

There were days when Dad couldn't even sit up straight in a chair, or lift the spoon to his mouth. He had no physical strength. It was hard to experience this deterioration with him, especially after having worked with him in my garden only three years before. He helped me dig out pathways and a pond. I couldn't keep up with his energy. He was so strong, then.

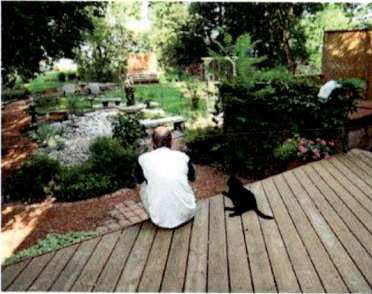

Dad worked with me in back-breaking work over a summer to transform our bleak back yard into a tranquil oasis: He & my cat, Taz, soaking up the beautiful results of our work - 2002

I struggled to contain my anger, with this new reality; to accept how this once virile man was being consumed by this horrible disease.

I remember baking Dad a cake on his 45th Birthday.

I was 15, and thought, "Wow, my dad is so old... I hope he lives 'til I graduate!"

In 1975, Dad was parenting a 15-year old "know-it-all" and still managed to smile!

Become the Man
You Want to Marry.

I remember one scene from my youth like it was yesterday: I was 15, in grade ten, and decided to quit school, with only 3 months left to final exams (I hadn't studied or done any work all year, so I didn't want to face the imminent failure).

I thought I knew everything I needed to know when I was 15, anyway, just like every other 15-year-old I knew!

I thought, "School certainly couldn't teach me anything that I didn't already know!"

When I came home – like a drama queen – and threw my books on the floor to announce that I was not returning to school, Dad took the news surprisingly well.

He said, "Well, **that's an adult decision that comes with adult consequences**. I'll give you a month to find a job, and then your room and board will be 35 dollars a week."

That was a lot of cash in 1975. It probably equates to at least $150 a week nowadays.

It also meant that I would lose my privileges to the car, the free gas, and my monthly allowance.

I ended up finding a job in a local pizza shop that summer, working for minimum wage. What fun that was! It was also an immediate awakening to the realities of life – having to manage my budget and quickly realize that there was always less cash than expenses every month.

It wasn't long before school seemed like a welcome alternative.

After that summer, I was the first one to register for the next semester!

My dad was a tough teacher as a single parent, but he always dished out his lessons in a loving and memorable way.

I remember him always telling me to **"become the man you want to marry."** It was important for him to instill the value of independence to us as young women.

Question Everything!

We had talked about death a few times. He always said he was "ready to go anytime."

We had talked about religion, too. He was born into a strict Catholic family with a matriarch who inflicted as much mental abuse as physical. It was an upbringing that would leave most people bitter, angry, and stuck in the past.

But Dad was always the most positive and enthusiastic person I knew. The only lingering scars were kept deep within him, which likely contributed to his ulcer and his alcoholism. His religious indoctrination didn't prevent him from wanting me to learn how to keep an open mind, explore other religions, and question everything.

Religion was something I started to question when I was 11 years old. When I told dad I didn't want to go to church anymore (because I didn't believe anything I was seeing, reading or hearing) he said I would have to make a compromise. The hour that would normally be spent in the Sunday ritual and obligation of attending church would now be spent with me reading and learning about another religion.

That lesson put me on a path of appreciating that all religions exist to control people (especially women) with social expectations and cultural conditioning that keep you stuck in a cycle of obedience, compliance, fear, uncertainty, and doubt. But I also appreciate that religions offer solace to people and provide a much-needed sense of community, connection, and belonging. That's a compromise I'm not sure I'll ever be able to make.

Towards the end of dad's life his religion became important to him, and that surprised me. It makes me wonder how I will evolve through my life process, and it makes me grateful that dad encouraged me to keep wondering about life, and keep questioning everything!

I've often wondered how dad's indoctrination may have contributed to his alcoholism, as I often wonder what factors may have contributed to mine. Dad's alcoholism was the kind that kept him functional for months at a time, but - when he did go on a bender - he would disappear for days and sometimes weeks. That's when I became more involved in his real estate business. I needed to field the incoming calls from clients and pretend that Dad was just "away" on business.

When he did finally come home from a bender, he didn't even look like my dad. He was pale and frail, and had all the battle scars of a bottle binge.

I would help him dry out, nursing him back to health with a bottle and a bucket. He would drink straight gin and then throw up. He drank until he stopped throwing up. It was a horrible experience for me. I can't imagine what it was like for him.

When I was 16, Dad had the worst binge ever. I received a call from a hospital in New York, saying that Dad was there and unable to pay his hospital bill. I needed to come up with nearly eight thousand dollars USD! That was a lot of money in 1976. That's when my real estate skills became evident, and I managed to raise the money by making and expediting a few sales.

There was one significant difference about this binge, though. When he was lying in bed, near death, he said, "Get me through this, sweetheart, and I'll never drink again." That was something I had never heard before, and he stayed true to his word.

My experience with alcoholism is an ongoing journey that has me in a current state of sobriety. I enjoy those "states" for months and sometimes years at a time, but then there are other "states" that have me sliding down the slope of sabotage that threatens my livelihood and my life.

Dad always used to say "alcoholism is a progressive disease, so be careful." After years of therapy, self-help programs, and AA indoctrination I'm still on the fence about the disease factor that's associated with alcoholism. Through all my "states" of sobriety and otherwise I've just learned to keep wondering about life, and keep questioning everything.

*Life is Like a
Roll of Toilet Paper…
the closer it gets to the end, the
faster it goes.*

Eventually, Dad could no longer live on his own, but wasn't ready to even consider moving into an extended care facility (we were careful to never say "nursing home").

Chantal had moved to Ontario a few years before, and purchased a home. She and Dad agreed to finish the basement into a self-contained apartment, so he could have relative independence but still be close enough for immediate assistance if needed.

Later that same year, Lance and I moved from Canada to Spain. It was a decision that was difficult to make, because I wanted to be near Dad while he made the frightening journey of slowly losing his mind.

I couldn't imagine my life without my family, because it was actually the first time we had all been together in the same province for many years.

I had moved from NS to BC when I was 18, and Chantal had spent a few years in Alberta after having Tyler. She eventually settled back in NS, but went to the mainland instead of our birthplace on Cape Breton Island.

I got married in 1991 to a British man I met in Cape Breton. I had been operating a small business there for a few years, and was actually in the process of selling it when I met Lance. My intention was to move back to BC, but those plans were derailed when I met the love of my life.

Lance had been married for 11 years, unhappily. His girlfriend had gotten pregnant when they were 18, and he did what any honourable young man did in those days. Over the course of their rocky marriage they had 3 children, and his wife had several affairs. He finally packed it in, filed for divorce, and found a job that brought him to my part of the world.

After we met and married in Nova Scotia, we moved to England, but it was short-lived. I only lasted 7 months there, before realizing that being a weekend mom was not what I wanted in life. Thankfully, being a weekend dad wasn't what Lance wanted either... so he followed me back to Canada.

We were living in Halifax when Chantal arrived back from Alberta. She had become pregnant while in university, and Tyler was born in 1989 when she was 21. Tyler was 2 when he was finally diagnosed with Williams syndrome. Chantal and Tyler's father tried to make it work together, but her stint in Alberta with him ended in 1992.

By that time, Lance and I had settled into a very small studio apartment in Halifax, NS, overlooking the harbour.

Chantal and Tyler moved in with us, and Chantal got a job at a bank.

Lance was unable to find a job, so he was able to babysit Tyler while Chantal and I worked.

Dad had retired to Florida, and was living in a mobile home park and seemed to be enjoying his retirement in a warm climate.

From the time I married Lance in 1991 to the time Dad was diagnosed with Alzheimer's in 2005, the years were simply filled with "life." We worked ⅓ of our lives, slept ⅓ of our lives, and tried to fill the other ⅓ of our lives with family and social events.

Lance and I moved to Spain in 2007, and Dad's health was deteriorating quickly. Chantal arranged to visit us with Tyler, Dad, and dad's former girlfriend of many years, Pat. It was December, so it was relatively chilly in Spain, and we were in the process of moving from one apartment to another so the 10-day visit passed far too quickly.

January 17/08 was my sister's 40th birthday, and I wished I could have been there to celebrate with her, especially because we had just received news that Dad's condition has advanced to the latest stages of Alzheimer's. He had a form of dementia called Lewy Body, which manifested in Parkinson's symptoms. He had been placed on the priority list for "extended care."

He didn't take the news very well. Although he was physically feeble, he was still mentally fine most days. It must have been excruciating for him to deal with his physical limitations. He could no longer wash or dress himself, and feeding himself was a challenge at times. Chantal or I often had to cut up his meat for him. To see a man who was so independent become so dependent was a horrible experience for all of us.

In March/08, dad had a serious fall while vacationing in the Dominican Republic with his best friend from his heyday. He was still lucid most days, so he was insistent that he and his best friend take one last trip together to sunny climes.

Dad ended up spending 3 days in the hospital there (it was apparently an uncomfortable and frightening experience for him because they restrained him to the bed!). He then spent another 2 days in a Toronto hospital after he came back to Canada. It was there that, thankfully, the ER doctor recommended 24/7 care, so dad was put on a priority list. He moved into a room at an extended care facility on March 18. I wanted to return to Canada to see him, but Chantal thought that would be too hard on everyone. Dad would feel guilty if I left Lance and my life in Spain. I fought the feelings of guilt for being so far away when I imagined that he must have been feeling the most vulnerable he has ever felt in his life.

I made the decision to return to Ontario on March 31, to stay until April 11. I needed to see Dad through this transition – his biggest fear – of ending up in a nursing home.

I stayed with Chantal & Tyler, and – even though the time was marking a sad event – we had a lot of great times together.

When dad was diagnosed with Lewy Body, he was living in Chantal's basement, which he had helped her renovate into a studio apartment.

Chantal decided to move Tyler into the basement apartment, and also decided that the small, studio space needed more storage (a time that we now laughingly call "our Ikea experience").

2008: Trip to Ikea turned Chantal's SUV into a Flintstone's ride!

I spent a lot of time with Dad during that visit, having lunch with him every day. The staff, facilities, and the food were all excellent. He seemed very happy there. In fact, he seemed to be handling the transition to this new lifestyle better than Chantal and I were handling it.

He was physically very frail, and could barely walk without the aid of a walker. If we wanted to take a day trip, we needed to take the wheelchair with us. His strength was diminishing quickly. He could no longer adjust his weight to lie comfortably in bed. He couldn't even swing his legs up on the bed from a sitting position.

I was thankful that we got to spend some quality time together. One day we went to Ikea to look for a small table and chairs for his "apartment." We borrowed the collapsible wheelchair from the facility, so Dad was comfortable for the long tour around Ikea. We had coffee in the cafeteria, and Dad had a HUGE cinnamon roll (his favourite). When we were returning to the car, he asked me how he was moving. I explained that I was pushing him in the wheelchair. He asked "But, how do I stop?" I stopped walking, and said "Like that." He said "How did I do that?" I explained that I was pushing him from behind. He didn't quite grasp the concept. It's moments like that which made me very sad for his experience... although, when you asked him... he said he was not fearful in any way. I'm not sure now if he even realized that he was asking such questions about relatively simple things.

Our goodbye was extremely sad for me. Dad never really showed his emotions at the best of times, so I'm not even sure he was grasping the fact that I was about to leave for Spain – again. This time, however, it would represent the last time we see each other.

Experience Comes From Bad
Judgement,
and
Good Judgement Comes
From Experience.

Mom was still a virgin at 21 when she married my dad. In those days, that's what women were expected to do... remain a virgin until you marry, have kids, and be a good wife and mother.

Mom and Dad, 1960

The problem is that **some women should never have children**. Some women are not suitable for motherhood. My mother was one of them, and so am I.

Thankfully, Mom married a man who was one-of-a-kind. When she ran off with the sailor, Dad stepped up to the plate to raise his 2 girls (in spite of everyone telling him to leave his mother or mother-in-law with the responsibility).

So, how does one resist falling into that cycle of social construct that is designed to make us do "what's expected?"

I think it helps if you can start your journey of self-discovery early in life. The earlier the better. Keep asking yourself, "What do I want?" And, most importantly, keep answering the question!

Learn to trust your instincts

Have you ever done anything you really didn't want to do? Something that you "knew" didn't feel right or didn't feel good... but you found yourself doing it anyway?

Making the decision to leave Canada and move to Spain was like that for me.

When the opportunity presented itself to move to Spain, it certainly made sense to move to a warmer climate sooner than later; instead of waiting until we retire (which is what we intended to do).

But, now here come the "buts."

But, we had just finished renovating our century home in rural Ontario, my real estate business was finally showing a profit after 3 years, and I was finally feeling "settled" for the first time in my life.

Chantal and Tyler were living close by, and Dad had moved from Florida to rent an apartment within walking distance of my house! It was sizing up to be a picture-perfect life, by all accounts.

But, my father had been recently diagnosed with Alzheimer's, and my sister was struggling to raise a special-needs son on her own while juggling the responsibilities of an ever-demanding job/career in human resources.

It was especially frustrating to arrive in Mallorca to feel less than welcome by the Spanish bureaucracy. It took me 18 months to fulfill the paperwork requirements in Spain, and many of those months had me wondering what the hell we had done in leaving our roots in Canada.

When I say "roots," I don't mean that literally. My husband, Lance, was born in England. We met in Canada, fell in love, got married, and lived in MY country together for 16 years before moving to Mallorca, Spain.

The opportunity to live and work in Spain was like a dream come true for us. We were at an age where the prospect of semi-retirement in a Mediterranean climate sounded spectacular. The reality of the move, however, proved to be a challenge from day one... a challenge that had me regretting the decision more often than not.

Lance would be working with his brother in a company that was growing fast. The brother's contacts in the yachting industry were impressive enough to launch a refurbishment company in Mallorca that served the second largest yachting port in Europe. Lance was hired as project manager, a role he mastered quickly. Things were going great, until the economy faltered in 2008 and the ripples rolled through even the deepest of pockets.

We returned to Canada in 2011, and I was greatly relieved. The reality of living in Spain was far from my imagined dream. The bureaucracy was infuriating, as was the native resentment of immigrants/ex-pats, and the general ignorant mentality of religious bias.

I returned to Canada with a whole new appreciation for a country that exemplifies compassion and diversity.

I was also relieved to be moving away from Lance's family. They never liked me – we had nothing in common – and the feeling was mutual. Actually, we did have one thing in common – our love for Lance. Poor Lance was always caught in the middle of two entities he loved dearly that didn't like each other! It was a losing situation for him, which I was happy to leave behind.

Truth:
A Fundamental Reality
Defined by a Person's
Perceived Experience.

Everybody's truth is different, that's for sure! When I initially wrote this part of the book, my father-in-law was still alive. He passed on in 2017, and I hope he's resting in peace... even though we couldn't stand being around each other for any length of time. Even on his death bed, I couldn't bring myself to wish him well and say goodbye.

I loved the scene from the sitcom Home Improvement when Tim, the Tool Man Taylor, told his eldest son – who wanted to go skiing with his friends over the Christmas holidays – "This is Christmas... a time to be with family, not with friends and people you like."

I can relate.

In 2014, I spent 2 months with my in-laws who came from the UK to spend Christmas with us in Canada. Yes, I realize now that it was unwise to ignore the houseguest rule: Houseguests are like fish... after 3 days they start to stink!

I think I'm a pretty likeable person, and I've rarely come across someone who didn't like me. That is, until I met my in-laws.

I'd been married to their son for 24 years when they came to visit us that Christmas.

Lance and I met in Canada while he was there on a working visit in 1991. He had been divorced for 2 years by that time, and he had 3 kids in the UK who were living with his ex-wife and the guy who had been having an affair with her for years (which was the reason for the divorce).

But, all that didn't matter. As far as his parents were concerned, I was still the homewrecker who stole their son away from his family.

My in-laws are the type of people who contribute to the creation of terms like "the outlaws."

They are typically British. They come from the patriarchal society and mentality where appearance is everything. Stiff upper-lip kind of thing, you know?

They are people I love (sort of?), *because they're family*. But, they are not people I like, or people I would ever choose to spend time with... and they all feel the same way about me, but pretend it's all *my fault* because I should be the one to try to "fit in."

They don't like me, but that's not something they would ever admit. They prefer to suffer in passive aggression, and poke a stab at me every now and again to remind me that I don't fit in with their family and that I don't try hard enough to fit their *"ideal of family."*

During that Christmas visit, his father actually said to Lance, "You should have married Jackie (the woman he was dating before he met me)... oh yes, that would have been a good marriage, and you would still be in England."

Yes, their beloved son would still be in England, if it hadn't been for me! Maybe they're right. I doubt it, though. My husband took the travelling job so he could heal his broken heart from being ripped away from his children by an adulteress. If he hadn't met me, I'm sure he would have eventually met someone else on his travels who didn't want to live in the UK.

What's really sad is that I nearly had fisticuffs with his 80-year-old mother... on my birthday!!! It was because I failed to open my birthday present "when it was expected." If my husband hadn't stepped between us, I think she would have actually hit me. Her seething dislike for me all these years had finally reared its ugly head. I was drunk at the time, though, so I'm sure that coloured my perspective.

My behaviour, drunk and sober, has always fallen short of my in-laws' expectations. They've never actually vocalized their expectations, mind you. It was just expected that I should know what their expectations were. I was supposed to be a mind-reader, and just behave the way they expected me to behave.

That's my truth – my *"perceived experience."*

It's Okay to Take a Dip in
the Pity Pool and Have a
Few Laps, but You
Eventually Have to
Get Out and Dry Off!

My marriage nearly ended during our stint in Spain, because we were living just one street away from my in-laws/his parents – who were feeding him animosity toward me every day for 4 years. It nearly drove me crazy!

I was ready to throw in the towel, and leave him to be with "his family." I figured it was probably for the best. Then, maybe everyone would be happy. Well, at least his parents would have definitely been happy, as would his kids and grandkids probably. He would finally be "back home."

I was really feeling sorry for myself.

My dad used to tell me, "It's okay to take a dip in the pity pool and have a few laps, but you eventually have to get out and dry off!" Oh God, how I miss my dad.

I can only imagine what my Philosopher Dad would say to me about this scenario, if he were still living in this realm.

He would say, "You are blessed to have found someone who loves you unconditionally. You are a princess upon whom he would lavish all the riches of the world. He loves you, and he loves his parents... two incompatible entities that hold equal importance to his life... but he's stuck in the middle and just wants everyone to be happy. He's a peacemaker. Cut him some slack."

My dad would be absolutely right. My husband adores me, and he's heartbroken that his parents dislike me and I them. If he could wave the magic wand of enchantment to make everyone happy, he would.

I'm grateful for Dad's advice, and I'm grateful I actually took it this time to save my marriage!

We Become
the Company We Keep.

Have you ever heard the expression, "After all I've done for you….?"

It usually comes from people who like to use a measuring stick in their lives to gauge their relationships.

I have learned that managing a relationship with a scoreboard doesn't work, because no-one can ever measure up to the subjectivity of another's calculations.

Thankfully, I've never heard anyone ever say to me "After all I've done for you," because I am selective with the company I keep. I make it a point to have people in my life who are generous with their time and attitude, and I treat everyone in my life with that same philosophy.

My Philosopher Dad was always saying "We become the company we keep," often reminding me that my choice of friends was questionable during my teenage years!

Dad also used to say, "Charity begins at home," and I was never quite sure what that meant – until I grew up/matured, and realized that charity is best realized and appreciated when it's practiced with our family and friends.

The idea of charity has been simplified to mean "donating" to a cause or less fortunate people. Charity, however, also means "generous actions."

I think that's the point my Philosopher Dad was making when he often recited this quote. Dad was one of the most generous people I knew, and he always taught me and my baby sister by example.

The other most generous people I know are my sister and my husband. I am forever grateful to have had a generous person like my dad in my life so that my only sister is, naturally, inherently generous.

When I met my husband 25+ years ago, I knew he was "the one" because he possessed the same generous quality that I had grown accustomed to through my dad's influence.

Being generous in our actions is the most important form of charity, to me at least. We are largely products of our environment, so – if we are immersed in an environment of generosity – we tend to become generous people.

Family and friends are the foundation of our existence, so it makes perfect sense to build and nurture the foundation that supports us on this journey of life.

If you have people in your life saying "After all I've done for you…," it might be a good time to reflect on why you have people in your life who are using a measuring stick to whack you with when you don't meet their expectations.

We become the company we keep, so strive to keep your company positive, kind, loving, supportive, and nurturing.

Plan For Tomorrow
but
Live For Today.

Planning for tomorrow is not generally something we're taught to do when we're young, but neither is living for today.

I was fortunate to have lessons in both areas of planning and living, early in life, from my Philosopher Dad. He always told me that "*All we ever have is today, so live it to the fullest*."

My father also used to tell me to "*Pay yourself first*." He encouraged me to save 10% of everything I made and put it in a savings account. He told me I'd never miss it, and that it would accrue interest over the years that would keep me in good stead. He was right.

But, like most kids, I didn't listen to my father's advice.

It wasn't until I was in my 40s that I started to appreciate the wisdom of my father, and started to regret not taking his advice 20 years earlier. But, hey, that's how life goes, right?! We all need to forge our future our own way, and reflect on how different things might have been if we had chosen a different path.

The one piece of advice I did take from my father was something he said to me when I was in my late teens. I was faced with a dilemma of not knowing what I wanted to do with the rest of my life after I graduated from high school. I had just barely passed my senior year, so I knew I wasn't academically inclined to pursue further education.

As I pondered my options and shared my frustrations about not knowing what I wanted to be when I grew up, my father told me that "Life is short – plan for tomorrow, but live for today!"

So, instead of taking the path of most of my peers to head off to university to pursue an Arts degree (and look for a husband), I chose to buy a one-way ticket to travel by train across Canada – coast-to-coast – from Nova Scotia to British Columbia.

It was a trip of a lifetime, and I ended up spending 2 years in Vancouver working as an executive assistant to the president of an oil and gas corporation. Part of my job was screening his calls to decide who would get through to him and who would be leaving a message. A stockbroker who called said he loved the sound of my voice. I thought he was just trying to woo me, but he actually offered me a job preparing and broadcasting his morning business report for a local radio station!

That opportunity launched my 22-year career in broadcast journalism (a dream that had been earlier quashed by a Catholic nun guidance counselor who told me that journalism was "no vocation for a lady").

My whole life has been a series of events that unfolded from my philosophy of "living for today."

I met my husband in the most unlikely of circumstances after my gay best friend met him in a bar. After realizing that he wasn't gay, he said "You have to meet my girlfriend because we have the same taste in men!"

I had been attending a training seminar in Toronto that week, so the last thing I felt like doing after my return home was going out socializing on the weekend, but my friend insisted. If I hadn't gone, I would never have met my prince, who has blessed my life in marriage and partnership for the past 25+ years.

Mainstream Media Have an Agenda!

I used to be a junkie. A news junkie!

I lived and breathed news, and I forged a long-time career as a broadcast journalist in mainstream media. My job was to *embellish* the facts, and sensationalize the headlines. The more sensational the better.

For the first 15 years, my vocation was my fuel. I was a junkie, and news was my fix. I was an addict.

Being immersed in bad news every day was taking a toll. It was slowly chipping away at my soul.

Being on the scene of the Swiss Air crash at Peggy's Cove in 1998 was the beginning of a mental meltdown for me. That was the psychic trigger that went off in my brain to say, "I CAN'T DO THIS ANYMORE!!!"

But, at that point, broadcasting was pretty much all I had ever done… it defined me. Even the mere thought of leaving the profession made me feel full of fear. If I didn't do this, what the hell would I do?

My ego kept screaming, "Who will you be, if you can't call yourself a journalist?"

Being a journalist impressed people, and it was really important for me to feel like I was important.

It wasn't an easy decision to leave a career that had defined me for my entire life at that time, but I knew that I could no longer be part of mainstream media with an agenda that perpetuates what I like to call the FUD factor (fear, uncertainty, and doubt).

So, let's touch on that for a moment: Mainstream media has an agenda to perpetuate fear, uncertainty, and doubt.

Yep! The agenda of mainstream media is to perpetuate the FUD factor… to hook the listener, increase ratings, sell advertising, and make shareholders happy.

We are programmed by mainstream media and advertising that we are never enough. We are never good enough, never slim enough, never smart enough, never rich enough, we are never enough… until we buy something to make us feel better, of course, which feeds consumerism and capitalism as we know it!

I want to give you an example of how powerful these messages are. My nephew, Tyler, is an adult with Williams syndrome — a neuro-developmental disorder that leaves him with mental and physical challenges. Although he is chronologically and biologically 29 years old, he is mentally a 5-year-old in many ways. When Tyler received an iPad for Christmas one year, he was very excited and disappeared into the rec room after dinner so he could watch YouTube on his new iPad.

At the writing of this book, YouTube is the second most watched medium in the world next to television, and if you've watched anything on YouTube recently you know that you have to opt out of the commercials after 5 seconds. But, more often than not now, you have to actually sit through a 30-second commercial before you can watch your chosen video.

So, after watching YouTube for about an hour, Tyler returned to the living room to announce that he had to "lose weight and remove all the hair from his chest."

THAT is the power of mainstream media/advertising. That is the power of embellishing the facts to perpetuate fear, uncertainty, and doubt, and feed consumerism.

I was prompted to start a positive media company in 2010, after my husband and I moved to Spain. I realized that when we were no longer subjected to mainstream media (by virtue of not being able to understand the messages we were hearing) we became much happier people.

Now, I'm sure being in a warm climate on the Mediterranean also contributed to this new-found serenity… but there was also a significant equation to our state of mind and being removed from the bombardment of negative messages from mainstream media and advertising!

It is estimated that we humans process about 70 thousand thoughts every day, and most of those thoughts are negative because they're being influenced by negative messages… not only from mainstream media, but also our family, our friends, and our co-workers.

It's essential that we be aware of what we're allowing into our mind. Our minds are like gardens. We plant seeds, and they grow when nurtured. If we don't tend the garden, weeds start to take over. I like to think of the weeds as all the negativity we let seep into our minds (very often without us even realizing it) … things like mainstream media messages that keep telling us we're never good enough until we buy something to make us feel better; also, negative song lyrics, negative television programs, and negative friends/relatives/co-workers.

Be aware of the stuff you're absorbing into your mind/your garden. Are you sowing good seeds? Are you tending the weeds?

I encourage everyone to take the diet that really works: a media fast. Don't watch, read, or listen to news, and FEEL how much your life improves!

*When Faced With a Road
To Take, Always Choose the
Road Less Traveled.*

Dad knew that helping his kids find their way in life meant leaving room for lots of experience that would eventually (and, hopefully) lead the way for us to make good choices in life.

I can only guess that the road was difficult to navigate for my dad as a single parent in the 60s, but his guidance and judgement led me and my sister to roads that were less traveled.

He taught us to take responsibility for all our decisions... good and bad.

He taught us that love is unconditional, especially through the bad decisions.

He taught us that bad decisions are usually expensive, and usually always teach us a valuable lesson.

He taught us that good decisions are usually fruitful, albeit far fewer than the many bad decisions that we're likely to make through life.

He taught us that life is a mixture of good and bad... joy/sorrow, triumph/tragedy, hope/despair, and we can't appreciate the good until we've appreciated and learned from the bad.

What prevents people from taking adventures?

I suspect that it may have something to do with fear; fear that is ingrained into our psyche from birth.

We are taught to seek security. We're told to stay in school, study hard, get good marks, be popular, pursue a sport, get a good education, get a good job, buy a good car, find a good mate, get married, buy a house, have kids, get better jobs, get better homes, earn more money, save for retirement, retire… and, then we die. That's pretty much the path we're encouraged to follow from the day we're born.

Messages from mainstream media contribute to that indoctrination, bombarding us with messages of inferiority. We're never good enough. We're never slim enough, rich enough, smart enough, hairless enough, attractive enough… we're never enough; until we buy something or take something that fills the void. It's a cycle of insanity that feeds consumerism and capitalism as we know it.

When I was in my teens, my Philosopher Dad gave me a book that changed the course of my life. The book is called *The Road Less Traveled* by M. Scott Peck.

My dad had watched a lot of people settle into their lives, and live on auto-pilot… following that pre-determined path from birth to death. Dad said they were often, inevitably, the people who ended up living a life of regret. He strived to not be that person who settled, and he urged his daughters to do the same.

When all my friends were going to university, I decided to travel the country coast-to-coast to pursue my dream of being a foreign correspondent (a journalist who travels and covers global events).

When all my friends were getting married and having kids, I was living my dream of being an entrepreneur – and refusing to settle for a man who didn't adore and respect me.

When all my friends were saving for retirement, I cashed in my retirement fund and sold everything to travel and live in Spain for a few years.

Taking the road less traveled has been an adventure that I wouldn't trade for all the security in the world.

So, why am I different?

It might have had something to do with being raised by a single father. There was an inherent level of insecurity involved with growing up without a mother and having a father who worked an average 60-hour week. When you raise yourself, you become pretty independent and somewhat obstinate.

But, I think my sister and I were very lucky to have a dad who strived to give us as many adventures as possible, and he always encouraged us to live life to the fullest.

Philosopher Dad always told us to take the road less traveled, take full responsibility for our lives, and never settle for a life on auto-pilot. He used to say, "If there's an opportunity, just say yes – and figure out the details later."

So, in honour of my Philosopher Dad... I encourage you to always just say YES, and figure out the details later. Always take the adventure. Always take the Road Less Traveled!

Learn to Master Your Mind
Because
If You Don't
Someone Else Will.

Mindfulness

My Philosopher Dad always encouraged me to learn something new every day, even if it was just a word.

Mindfulness is a noun that means the state of being aware. In psychology, it's a technique that Eckhart Tolle wrote about in *The Power of Now*: focusing on the present to experience our feelings with awareness and without judgement.

What does mindfulness mean to you?

When I asked my husband what mindfulness meant to him, "caring" was his answer. He's an old soul who lives a compassionate and considerate existence, so I wasn't surprised by his answer.

Our fundamental reality is based on our perceived experience, and ***everyone's perception is different***. That's what makes life fascinating, I think. Several people can have the same experience, but each one of us will have our own perception of that experience.

In my ongoing quest for self-knowledge, I like to study the philosophy and lives of notable prophets. In ancient Greece, Socrates was known for saying "*Know thyself.*"

Self-examination is not a task that many of us have the courage to undertake, and it's generally not a journey that is encouraged during our formative years. From birth, we are immediately defined by our gender, and expected to fulfill the role of "being" male or female. Our lives are completely different, by default, by virtue of our gender!

We are then placed on the corresponding path of that gender, living on auto-pilot, conforming to societal norms. Anyone who is perceived as being on a journey of self-discovery is often criticized – and often labelled things like "different, new-age, artsy-fartsy, bohemian, eclectic."

Let's talk about the labels we put on others and ourselves.

There have been countless experiments done on water. One of the most famous experiments was conducted by Dr. Masaru Emoto, and demonstrated that a label placed on a container of water can actually change the molecular structure of the water!

Dr. Emoto took microscopic pictures of frozen water crystals.

A label of 'Thank You' turns the water crystal into a beautiful snowflake-like image.

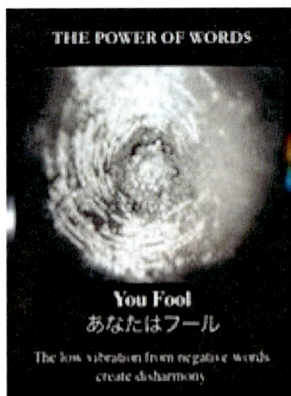

A label of 'You Fool' turns the same water source into an ugly, murky mess!

I really want you to think about this. We humans are comprised of almost 70% water... so what do you think the social "labels" are doing to us and our molecular structure?

Words are powerful. They can build us up, or tear us down. That's why I'm passionate about positive media.

It's important to filter what we allow into our minds. Our minds are like a garden. If we neglect it, weeds set in to overtake it and create a heck of a lot more work for us to clear that crap away! It's important to be aware and "**mindful**" of the seeds we are planting in our garden, and how we are tending our garden. How are you treating your mind?

So here is a question I'd like you to ponder. ***What do I want?***

The answer is important, because it will help you understand yourself better and help you get more control over your life.

Knowing thyself is the bottom line of mindfulness.

We always have a choice. We can either have life happen *to us*, or have life happen *for us*. Are you going to live on auto-pilot, or *BE the pilot*?!

So I challenge you to ask that question daily, and wait for the answer. When it comes, write it down. The answers are always an avenue for growth.

And always... please remember to take the diet that really works: a media fast. Don't watch, read, or listen to news and FEEL how much your life improves!

The Mosaic of Life

I was once asked to define and write an article about what mosaic means to me.

A dictionary.com definition tells us it's a noun that means several different things:

- Coloured pieces of glass/stone that make a picture or decoration
- Something that resembles such a picture/decoration made up of diverse elements i.e. a mosaic of borrowed ideas
- An aerial mosaic made up of aerial photographs to represent a geographical area

My favourite definition of mosaic in dictionary.com: In an architectural plan, it's a system of patterns for differentiating the areas of a building *or the like* – sometimes consisting of purely arbitrary patterns used to separate areas according to function.

When I think of mosaic, I think of people representing/ exhibiting arbitrary patterns used to separate areas according to function.

I am essentially an introvert who exhibits social attributes/behaviours in order to function efficiently in business and to form friendships and alliances.

Like most people, I thrive on connection to community, friends, and family. My patterns of behaviour change to accommodate the function. Do yours?

That's not to say that I am not fundamentally the same person in every different function I carry out in my daily life, but I do customize my behaviour and personality to different functions. I think it's a necessity for me to live harmoniously in all areas of my life.

An example of how I customize my behaviour to perform a function: While writing, I love to sit in front of my computer with my legs crossed in an almost half-lotus position (so my right ankle is resting on top of my left thigh near the knee, or vice-versa... I switch it up frequently). It's a very comfortable sitting/stretching position for me, because I have sciatica and it's a good way to stretch out the piriformis muscles...and it's also why I almost always choose to wear pants.

I sat like that once while I was hosting a current affairs show on television, interviewing a local politician. The feedback from the show was deafening, and it had nothing to do with the content of the interview. Everyone who commented said, "Why do you sit like that? It's not lady-like to sit like that!" So, I modified my behaviour to conform to society's expectation that women are supposed to sit a certain way. That doesn't change who I am; it changed my behaviour to function more successfully in the medium of television (and it also helped my decision to not appear on television anymore).

In life we are expected to conform to society's expectations of behaviour.

I've been a student of personal development and life-long learning for many years, and I know the objectives for me on this journey of life are basically to:

- learn to love yourself
- be kind to yourself and others
- treat others as you wish to be treated
- develop and practice a life motto of guiding values
- push yourself out of your comfort zone
- learn something new every day

While contemplating the writing of this article, I did a google search for "mosaic" and came across The Mosaic Institute in Toronto, whose motto is "Harnessing Canada's Diversity for Peace at Home & Abroad." The Mosaic Institute is a "think and do" tank that harnesses the diversity of Canada's people to build a stronger, more inclusive Canada, and **promote peace** all around the world. I encourage you to get their newsletter at https://mosaicinstitute.ca.

That's what I love about people. Our diversity.

That's also what I love about Canada. Our diversity, and our example to the world that we all possess unique patterns that combine to make an extraordinary mosaic that represents our connectedness.

I still feel connected to people who judge me for the way I sit, or the way I dress, or the way I speak and express myself. I appreciate that letting go of judgement is a process of personal development, and it's a process that few people have the courage to pursue. If it was easy, everyone would do it, right!?

Embrace Life!
Say YES to
Adventure
and
Experience,
and Figure Out
the Details Later.

I quit school in grade 10, for a multitude of reasons. The primary reason, though, was that I hadn't done any work all year and I knew that I was going to fail final exams. There were only 3 months left to the school year, and I quit.

I came home one day – like a drama queen – and announced to my dad, "I'm not going back there; there's nothing relevant for me to learn there."

My dad made an immediate decision that taught me a valuable lesson about life. I had to get a job and pay room and board for as long as I chose to not go to school.

He stuck to his plan, too! I paid him $35.00 a week for what felt like a year – and what felt like most of my pay.

I also lost other privileges – like using my dad's car, which always had a full tank of gas. I could still use his car, but I had to pay for the gas now.

I think I was the first person to enroll for school in the fall. I had to repeat grade 10, but I transferred to the general business program so I could at least learn some useful business skills like typing and bookkeeping.

I still wasn't sure what I wanted to do for the rest of my life when I was finally in grade 12. Being in high school was an experience I didn't enjoy, so it felt like it was a very long time! It was frustrating to not have an "ah ha" moment of what I wanted to do with my life in those few years that felt like an eternity.

What I did know was that I wanted to travel, and I was a news junkie at the time… so I figured that being a foreign correspondent would be a good way to travel the globe and cover the world's events as a journalist.

When I told my guidance counselor the plan, she (a Catholic nun) said, "Oh, no dear, that's no vocation for a lady."

One sentence from someone in authority derailed that dream for me.

A few weeks later, my grade 12 science teacher addressed the graduating class one day by saying, "I guess all you gals who haven't found yourselves a husband yet will be going on to university."

Unfortunately – as biased and offensive as that statement was – there was an element of truth to it.

Most of my female friends were going to university to pursue an Arts degree... and party... and have sex... and – maybe – find a husband.

I didn't have any interest in arts, getting drunk, having sex, or finding a husband. I got drunk in high school – a lot. I also had sex... not a lot, but enough to get pregnant in grade 12. I chose to have an abortion. It was a one-night-stand situation, and I didn't want to be pregnant in high school. I had seen a few of my friends go through that experience, and I knew it wasn't an experience I wanted to have.

I wanted to travel. I wanted to see and experience the world.

So, instead of going to university, I decided to buy a one-way ticket from the East coast of Canada to the West coast of Canada. It was the trip of a lifetime. In retrospect, I wish I had kept a detailed journal, instead of just relying on my memories. It was an amazing experience.

When I finally arrived in Vancouver, after a cross-country train trip that was epic, I hopped into a cab and said, "Take me to an inexpensive apartment-hotel in the downtown area, please."

OMG, I was so naive.

It wasn't until weeks later that I realized I was in a hotel that was largely frequented by "working girls."

Coming to Vancouver from a place like Cape Breton, I just thought Vancouver was a really friendly place (male drivers waved at me and cars honked their horns, while I was waiting for the bus every morning outside the hotel).

Naivety aside, my 2 years spent living in Vancouver taught me a multitude of things that I would likely never have learned in university.

I got a great job as the executive assistant to the president of an oil & gas corporation (a job that – today – I wouldn't dream of taking, now that I've matured and chosen to align myself with socially and environmentally-conscious companies and people). But, at the time, it was a great job with great pay for a young girl just out of high school.

I met some amazing people, and shared apartments with young women who helped me navigate the challenges of being a small-town girl growing up in a big city.

I also launched what would become my successful broadcasting career that would nurture me for the next 22 years.

There will always be a multitude of reasons and a multitude of naysayers to derail you from your dreams. Stay true to what you really want and who you really are.

Pay attention to your intuition. It's always trying to communicate with you. All you have to do is listen, and act.

Beware of the
FUD Factor

From infancy, we are programmed to assimilate to society. It starts with our gender. We learn to associate our identity with being male or female, and fall into the corresponding roles that go along with that gender... roles that are defined by society, schools, religion, family, and peers.

Our roles are then further defined by messages we hear throughout our lives. We process about 60-70,000 thoughts per day, conservatively. Most of those thoughts are negative.

If you are lucky to have a loving and supportive family, you may be able to offset many of those negative messages and thoughts. But, then you're exposed to all the negative messages from advertising and mainstream media. We are inundated with messages that we're never good enough, smart enough, attractive enough, rich enough, or thin enough.

We're encouraged to buy things to fill the void that's deliberately dug away by negative mainstream media messages.

Negative self-talk and labels that we place on ourselves are extremely destructive to our health and happiness.

Mainstream media have an agenda to perpetuate what I like to call the FUD Factor (fear, uncertainty, and doubt). When you keep hearing sensational headlines and embellished facts from news, the FUD Factor becomes your reality. You are in a constant state of anxiety and stress which can play havoc with your health. Here are a few things you can do that might help:

1. Take a media fast. When you don't watch, read, or listen

to negative news/messages and advertising you will feel an immediate difference to your biology.

2. Keep your company positive. Hang around with people who lift you up, motivate and encourage you. The sooner you ditch the negative naysayers in your life the better.

3. Be mindful of your self-talk. When you catch yourself saying or thinking something negative hit your reset button and switch to a positive word/thought. TALK TO YOURSELF LIKE YOU'D TALK TO YOUR BEST FRIEND.

If You Don't
Value Yourelf
Nobody Else Will!

My Philosopher Dad always used to tell me, "If you don't value yourself, nobody else will!" It didn't really resonate with me when I heard it the first time... but I was only 20 then.

He said it while I was considering lowering my commission on a real estate listing.

My dad and I worked together as a real estate sales team in the 80s, when mortgage interest rates were averaging 20% and the real estate market was lean and mean – in more ways than one!

My dad was the Real Estate Broker. I was the Sales Representative.

Dad was an excellent teacher and mentor, and taught me that people will always negotiate the best deal "for them." Fair enough, I thought. So I just needed to learn how to negotiate the best deal "for me." That's sales. That's commerce. That's capitalism. That's the reality of the world in which we live.

As a sales representative in real estate, it was my job to get the best price for my client – the seller. In return for my sales, marketing, and negotiating skills I charged the seller a commission for procuring that sale.

My Philosopher Dad used reality to convey to me a system that is really pretty simple: NOTHING happens in the world without salespeople, so they are a valuable commodity that should be revered – not ridiculed.

But, salespeople tend to be ridiculed. Why do you think salespeople have such a bad reputation? Where did it start? The Fuller Brush salesmen? Car salesmen? Insurance salesmen? The peddlers who would walk the streets in a trench coat lined with sub-standard products, and flash the open coat to passersby with a "Wanna buy a……?"

Like anything, the bad stories and experiences of people being manipulated or cheated in sales tend to drown out the multiple good stories and good experiences that people have with sales. When people have a good experience, they might tell a couple of people.

When people have a bad experience, they tend to tell everyone they meet.

The majority of salespeople, in this century at least, invest LOTS of time and money to educate themselves, pretty much the same way lawyers, doctors, plumbers, engineers, and teachers do. So, why is the measuring stick different? What makes the education of a lawyer, doctor, plumber, engineer, or teacher any better – or different – than the education of a sales professional?

My Philosopher Dad had the answer for me.

Institutions are created to fulfill a mandate this is devoted to the promotion and endorsement of the members who subscribe to that mandate.

The perceived value of that promotion and endorsement is set and perpetuated by the members who enlist governments and corporations to recognize *their* piece of paper as being more valuable than someone else's piece of paper.

Educational institutions have become business enterprises that sell a commodity, and like any commodity the value is determined by market conditions and the strength of the institutions providing the commodity... and the connections of the institutions to keep the market value high.

So, what's your piece of paper worth?

I have LOTS of skills that I have learned, developed, and honed over the years, and I have LOTS of paper.

The only difference is that all of those skills and all of that paper have come from different institutions.

That's how I learned to value myself.

Learning to value and love ourselves is one of the most challenging things in life to learn.

It definitely helps if we have parents, teachers, and peers who encourage us. More often than not, though, we end up looking outside of ourselves to fill a void that wasn't filled in childhood. Sometimes that can result in addictions, a series of bad relationships, or a job that doesn't feed and fuel our talents.

I was fortunate to have the "value" lesson early in life... however, the "love" lesson took a bit longer. I think that's because I spent so long in a career that immersed me in negativity every day.

When we expose ourselves to mainstream media, we are exposing ourselves to messages that are constantly negative... . we are never good enough, thin enough, smart enough, rich enough – and on and on and on. We are manipulated into buying things that promise to make us feel better. That's sales. That's commerce. That's capitalism. That's the reality of the world in which we live.

It's no wonder that learning to love ourselves can be challenging in a world that tells us we are never enough.

When I founded *The Good News Only* in 2010, my mission was to spread positive media in the world and to provide resources of good news to prove that there are far more good things and far more good people in the world than bad.

That's why I always encourage everyone I meet to "Take the diet that really works: a media fast. Don't watch, read, or listen to news and FEEL how much your life improves!"

What is Success?

Do you consider yourself to be successful?

What is your definition of success? Do you have a clear definition of what success means to you? Because, if you're using someone else's definition of success to apply to your own life, chances are you might not be feeling very successful.

I remember hearing an interview with John Paul Getty, when he became one of the first billionaire's in the world. John Paul Getty was an industrialist, a very wealthy man... and when he became a billionaire a reporter asked him, "so, how does it feel to be one of the world's first billionaire's?" and he replied, "well, you know, a million dollars doesn't go as far as it used to!"

Obviously, John Paul Getty's definition of success looks a lot different than most people's definition of success. It's important to have your own definition, so you're not setting yourself up for disappointment and feelings of failure.

I like to define success differently for different areas of my life.

I have a clear definition of success when it comes to my material abundance, and a different definition of success when it comes to love and relationships. I also have a different definition of success for my spirituality or higher consciousness, and a different definition of success for my health and well-being.

I encourage you to have clear definitions of success for different areas of your life so you know what success feels like for you, instead of comparing your life to someone else's definition of success.

Bad Things Happen, Even to Good People!

"Bad things happen in life so the faster you accept that the better," my Dad used to tell me. He didn't say it to be hurtful or sarcastic. He just wanted me to learn to take personal responsibility for my life, and to understand that bad things will happen in life... even to good people.

Dad was a man of few words, but his words always made a lasting impression.

When I was 18 my father gave me a book written by Harold Kushner, *When Bad Things Happen to Good People*. Kushner was a rabbi who lost his 14-year old son to an incurable disease, and he wrote the book to reflect on a question that many of us ask: **"If we live in a universe governed by a God – one who we presume to be a God of a good and loving nature – than why is there so much suffering and pain?"**

What I learned from that book is that life is a series of events governed largely by our choices – and there will always be circumstances that will be beyond our control, like death.

My Dad was diagnosed with Alzheimer's shortly after he retired. Our family became thankful that he lived a full and happy life, and grateful that he didn't linger too long in that horrific disease. The anniversary of his death just passed recently, and the sadness will always be with me. Life will never be the same without him, but my life goes on.

Life's "bad things" can certainly leave us wondering why a universe governed by a loving God would have us feeling any pain and suffering.

And, what if you don't believe in God or a Higher Power?

From the point of view of an atheist (my husband), we are basically animals with a purpose to survive and procreate.

Based on the history of our planet, it is our destiny to become extinct.

But, as human animals, we have evolved into *sentient beings* who contemplate the big questions of **"why are we here, and what is our purpose?"**. We have either been born into religious dogma, or gravitated toward something outside of ourselves that helps us navigate the meaning of life. Our beliefs, religious or otherwise, normally dictate how we will deal with the bad things that happen in our lives.

Being highly social animals, we have also evolved into families and communities that bond us in this thread of life and help us move forward through our grief and struggle to accept all the bad things that happen in our lives, including the passing of our loved ones.

So I often find myself reflecting on my dad's words all those years ago: "*Bad things happen in life so the faster you accept that the better.*"

We are the sum total of our life's decisions. When we make bad decisions – that inevitably result in consequences – it's **how we choose to deal with those negative results** that will ultimately define the quality of our lives. It basically comes down to either seeing the glass half-full, or half-empty. It's a choice.

I am grateful to my father, my *Philosopher Dad*, who instilled the value of taking personal responsibility for my life, and for gifting me with not only his wisdom but also the wisdom of countless other visionaries and philosophers who all echo a similar message: *We may not immediately appreciate how failure can lead to success, or how loss can contribute to our future growth, but we grow to learn that failure and loss actually makes us stronger – if we choose to not keep swimming in the pity pool*.

SO, WHETHER YOU BELIEVE IN A HIGHER POWER OR NOT, HERE'S HOPING THAT YOU'RE CHOOSING TO SEE ALL THE GLASSES IN YOUR LIFE AS FULL.

*Beware of
The FUD Factor…
Always*

FIFTEEN YEARS AFTER 911, THE JIHADIST THREAT LOOMS LARGER THAN EVER ACROSS THE GLOBE

This was a headline that ran on the front page of the Washington Post in 2016.

The Washington Post was recently cited by a "journalist" (who was being interviewed by Chelsea Handler) as a "reliable source of information."

The headline is untrue, and the journalist should know better than to perpetuate American propaganda.

The biggest threats across the globe are governments that are not being held accountable for balancing budgets, protecting our environment, and creating sustainable jobs. But, nobody seems to want to write, read, or talk about that. Instead, the public is broadsided with headlines and sensational stories that keep you embroiled in dialogues that are unhealthy and unproductive.

Virtually everything we watch, read, and hear these days is controlled by just a few American conglomerates with an agenda to perpetuate the FUD Factor (fear, uncertainty, and doubt).

Remember, objective evidence is manipulated by mainstream media to invoke fear, uncertainty, and doubt; and "news literacy" is subjective, so make sure you're being informed by reliable sources!

Humanity will not evolve until the conversation deepens, so let's start insisting on deeper, truthful, factual, solutions-based conversations.

Nix the Negativity

Sometimes the negative natter that picks away at our brain can be deafening, and it can often keep us stuck in a negative rut that's hard to climb out of.

The good news is that negative thinking doesn't have to be a hard habit to break.

One of the best places to start is by taking a media fast (the diet that really works!). I know I'm sounding like a broken record, but – please trust me on this – when you don't watch, read, or listen to news (and advertising) you'll FEEL how much your life improves.

How Will A Media Fast Help You?

When you filter out the negative messages from mainstream media, you will become the gatekeeper of your mind. When you are the wise protector of your mental space, you will start to feel more empowered, more confident, more willing to stand up for what you want in life. Start treating your mind like you'd treat a garden. When you plant good seeds, and nurture them, good things grow.

Play the Opposite Game

Instead of letting your internal commentator be fed and controlled by advertising and other mainstream media, you can throw it a curve by coming up with the complete opposite of what the commentator is yelling at us. For example: When it says, "He's such a jerk for cutting me off in traffic (or cutting in line)," you can say, "He's got so much on his mind that he is totally oblivious to everyone around him, poor guy!"

Or, when it says, "This job sucks and I can't stand working with all these toxic, self-centered people every day!," you can say, "I am so grateful that this job provides a good living, is teaching me something about myself every day, and is – therefore – a growth opportunity!"

When you choose to play the game of opposites, the positive self-talk commentator voice overcomes the negative voice, and it can become a healthy habit to make you feel better – both mentally & physically.

Put on Your Rose-Coloured Glasses

Now that you're getting good at the opposite game, you can start to look for examples of when it's actually true! It's a pretty good bet that you'll find at least one example, however small it is. When you find it, build on it. Let it warm your heart. Let it restore your faith in humanity. Let it grow in your mind's garden. Who were you with? What did they say? How did you feel? What did you do? The longer you think about it, and FEEL it, the more it sinks into your subconscious to start changing the mental frameworks that used to see the world through gray-tinted lenses. The neurotransmitters of our mind change with our thoughts. When we consistently make the effort to keep our thoughts positive, our brain creates new neuro-pathways of positivity.

Decide on Your Next Action

Now that you realize how you are being manipulated by mainstream media, you can start making better choices about what you are allowing into your mind. You can start being more selective about how you spend your time and who you spend your time with. Are your friends supportive and encouraging? Are there other factors in your life that could be contributing to negativity?

Remember, we become the company we keep and the thoughts we absorb, so it's important to keep both our company and our thoughts as positive as possible.

The Insanity of
Marketing Madness

In 2005, a now-defunct travel company enlisted an endorsement from a psychologist to identify the "most depressing day of the year."

It was done as a marketing gimmick to induce more travel during the winter months!

In order to manipulate the masses into believing that his opinion had merit, the quack doctor developed a pseudo-scientific formula that factored in things like the average weather conditions, average debt levels, and low motivational levels.

The "formula" has no basis in science and has since been debunked by mental health professionals, but "Blue Monday," (the third Monday of January) has taken on a life of its own. Unfortunately, #BlueMonday has even become a trend on twitter.

People are now, at least, being encouraged to use the day to reflect on things that really matter in their lives. It has also morphed, thankfully, into a way to broach the taboo topic of mental illness in general.

So, when January rolls around and you start to feel melancholy because you're listening to media messages that tell you it's "normal to feel that way," there are ways that you can infuse your days with more joy and happiness.

Here are just a few small actions you can take to help give blues the boot:

Make Happiness Your Goal

You are the sole person responsible for making yourself happy. Think about that word "responsibility" – RESPONSE + ABILITY.

It's important to remember that it's not necessarily WHAT happens to us that matters, but rather HOW we react to what happens to us that matters.

Your ability to respond positively to your choices often determines your satisfaction and happiness. Likewise, when we respond negatively to our choices, we're more likely to be dissatisfied and unhappy.

Does it make sense to choose to be around people who are enthusiastic, positive, and inspirational – and to make a conscious effort to choose environments that will bring peace, comfort, and joy to your life?

Know Your Core Values

Core values are the things that make us who we are. Unearthing your core values can improve the quality of your life and help you live with purpose.

Does your life reflect the values that are most important to you?

How do you discover your core values?

One way to start contemplating and developing your core values is to visit the University of Pennsylvania's website, Authentic Happiness (https://www.authentichappiness.sas.upenn.edu/testcenter), where you can register a profile and take the VIA Survey of Character Strengths questionnaire.

Speak the Truth

Very few people speak assertively, because it's a difficult thing to do – skillfully. Sometimes an assertive comment can ruffle a few feathers on people. So many people, instead, speak passive-agressively and often make their wants known in jokes or off-side remarks. Speaking assertively is a crucial skill that's worth honing. The key is knowing what you want, believing you have a right to it, and finding the courage to express yourself respectfully. If you do end up ruffling a few feathers, consider that it's probably a flock worth avoiding.

Relish the Moment

When you stop to take notice of the GOOD things around you, you can cultivate more optimistic thinking. Take time to enjoy a sunset, walk your dog, or share a laugh with a friend. The key is to take time to appreciate it and celebrate it for as long as possible. Savour the moment and linger in the feeling of optimism.

Feel & Express Gratitude

Gratitude is crucial in creating and maintaining happiness. It helps you focus on all the GOOD things in your life and all the great things that you already have, instead of stressing about what you don't have and concentrating on negative things.

Remember, your thoughts are currency for creating whatever you want in life, so when you pick positive thoughts you'll create positive things.

Here are a few more of my Philosopher Dad's quotes:

"Worry is the interest you pay
on a debt that never comes due."

"Two wrongs don't make a right."

"If you're going to do something,
do it right the first time."

"Nobody on their death-bed ever wishes
they'd spent more time at work."

"Never change yourself to make someone else happy.
Only change yourself to make yourself happy!"

"If you're the smartest person in the room,
go to a different room."

"Pursue your passion and the money will follow."

"Personal responsibility is paramount
to a good life."

"The first one to get angry loses."

"Learn something new every day."

"Buy the highest quality you can afford
so you only have to buy it once in your lifetime."

"Pay yourself first. You won't miss 10% of your income,
and it will add up quickly!"

"Tackle the things you least like to do
first thing in the morning
so the rest of your day is enjoyable."

"The most important skill you can develop is
to train and manage your mind."

Want to know a SECRET?

Unfortunately, the industry of personal development/self-help has been stigmatized by books/movies like *The Secret.*

While *The Secret* was great to bring attention to the power of our mind, it also commercialized, and somewhat trivialized, a scientifically proven universal phenomenon... *that energy is everything, and everything is energy.*

We are vibrating beings emitting "energy" at all times.

Have you ever walked into a room and said to yourself, "Wow, this place has bad vibes?" Have you met someone who you thought/felt was giving off a negative or positive vibe? Did it take long for you to reach that conclusion?

Your energy/vibe immediately reacts to the energy/vibe around you, and it will make you feel one of two things...either negative, or positive.

A vibe is simply a mood or a feeling. How often do we have a mood or a feeling? ALWAYS.

So, how do you Mind Your Mind?

Keep your company positive

We become the company we keep, so strive to keep your company positive. Align yourself with like-minded people, and limit your exposure to negative people who love to tell you about everything that's wrong in the world.

Keep your thoughts positive

We're bombarded with tens of thousands of messages daily – most of which are negative, and many of those thoughts include negative self-talk.

A few recommendations to keep things positive:

- Download music with positive and upbeat lyrics
- Watch movies that have an uplifting and positive message
- Listen to podcasts from people with positive messages to share
- Take the diet that really works: a media fast. Don't watch, read, or listen to news and FEEL how much your life improves.

Minding our Mind is a process that takes *deliberate strategy and action*. It's a **choice** that is guaranteed to improve the quality of your life.

All the great philosophers echo the same message: We can either be a servant to our mind, or the master of our mind.

We may not always get what we want, but we will always get what we vibrate.

You Become the Company You Keep, So Strive to Keep Good Company.

Difficult People in Your Life?

We humans are the most social animals on the planet, and relationships are the pathway to our wellbeing.

Positive relationships feed our need to bring meaning and happiness to our lives, and to become the best people we can be. Positive relationships help societies flourish, and organizations succeed.

And then there are the negative ninnies in our lives that can suck us into behaviours that are unhealthy and unproductive. Dysfunctional relationships can cause daily stress and leave us feeling drained and frustrated by a person's inability (or unwillingness) to collaborate and compromise for the greater good.

There's a memorable quote from French philosopher Sartre, who said, "Hell is other people."

So, let's look at a couple of questions:

1. What makes someone a difficult person?
2. How can we deal with them?

Spin Your Own Story

You've likely heard the adage: "Everyone has a story." So, instead of believing that a difficult person's sole purpose in life is to make yours miserable, it's healthier to assume that these people are dealing with their own crap in life. Start believing that their toxic attitudes and behaviours are merely consequences of past hurts that haven't healed. When your tyrant becomes a victim in your mind, it's easier to empathize.

Limit Your Exposure

Do what you can to limit your time spent with difficult colleagues. There is no need to initiate a conversation just because they walk into the kitchen while you're filling up your water bottle. If they engage you in conversation that's negative, just politely excuse yourself and LEAVE. It's tempting to try to socially connect with people by commiserating in their drama, but it's always best to avoid getting embroiled in unproductive dialogue.

Look After Yourself

Remember, emotions are contagious – both negative and positive! Be aware of your feelings and pay special attention to what helps you feel energized and positive. Positive psychology recommends a 3-1 ratio of good thoughts to bad, so be generous with yourself and the time you spend engaging in things that make you feel good about yourself.

Seek Support

There is no need to suffer in silence when you're dealing with difficult people. Seek out the company of like-minded people who are high with emotional energy and positive pursuits. Positive people will help you alleviate the stress of negativity and maintain a healthy perspective.

The Last Resort

If you've tried everything to offset the toxic titan in your life and still feel defeated, it might be time to change jobs. Just remember that difficult people are everywhere, unfortunately! The best approach is to avoid them whenever possible, and reappraise their behaviour when you can't.

Is There a Lesson?

It would seem that positive psychology and Sartre both have it right. If we allow toxic people to consume us and drive us to negative behaviours, then people can surely become our hell. But, if we don't seek out and nurture relationships that help us feel loved and appreciated, we will undoubtedly suffer and spread suffering... which will make us toxic people! We become the company we keep, so strive to keep your company and your environment as positive as possible.

F E A R
False Evidence
Appearing
Real

How Do You Handle Fear?

It's a perfect acronym for FEAR – False Evidence Appearing Real – because that's pretty much the basis of fear... it's false evidence that appears real to us at a specific time. What false evidence, you ask? Well, let's start with all the mainstream media messages that have us believing the world is full of trickery and terrorism. And, let's remember all those advertising messages that keep telling us we're never good enough.

While some fear can be healthy (it's always a good idea to avoid/escape any life-threatening scenarios), most fear is just a built-in defence that kicks in whenever we dare to think of what we truly want in life (our desires).

Have you dreamed about starting a new business where you can tap into your creativity? Maybe you've been wanting to write a book that's been simmering in your mind for a long time, or perhaps you'd like to change something in your relationship.

Instead of honouring our dreams and working toward them, we end up working toward shrinking them into the reality of our comfort zone. Why is that??? It's because our mind functions on learned behaviours from the past, based on experiences that we, or those around us, have had. Hence, the best predictor of future behaviour is past behaviour.

The good news is you can change it!

Know Yourself

Awareness is key. When you feel your defensive bodily response, be aware of what triggered it, and take note of the mental chatter that's feeding it. Knowing that it exists for a reason is essential to creating space from it. Remind yourself that you've grown from your past experiences, and your circumstances have changed. Take a short, mindful moment to help ground yourself in your current reality and allow yourself to open up to your desires.

Identify Your Defence

The best way to be true to our desires is to work backward from our defences. How do you react when a purpose speaks to your heart? Do you feel an urge to run away, or a flood of mental justifications – like how you're not good enough, competent enough, or presentable enough? Or perhaps that it's not the right time, right work, or right fit? Remember, all of these thoughts are self-focused and fed by the FUD Factor (fear, uncertainty, and doubt) that's perpetuated by mainstream media/advertising messages! The best way to counter these negative thoughts is to look beyond yourself to the difference you will make to others – *if* you were to follow your heartfelt desires.

Create an Action Plan

In this less fearful state, you're ready to plan the steps you'll take toward turning your dream into reality. Again, work backward with timelines and milestones. What action steps do you need to take to reach each milestone? When will you take them? Who will keep you accountable? And who will support you through your struggles, and celebrate your successes with you? The more specific you can be, the better your chances of fulfilling your dreams and desires.

Build Your Inner Resources

Remember, fear is part of our biological inheritance. It's what we have in common with every other creature on the planet. But what sets us apart is the ability to set and pursue goals, to visualize a better future, and the desire to make a positive difference in the world.

It's important to feed yourself a steady diet of inner resources that will keep you on your path to success and buffer you from the intrusions of your defence response. Stay focused on all the times you've risen up to life's challenges, all the things you've accomplished, and all the experiences that have helped you become resilient.

It also helps to take a media fast.

How Do You Handle Stress?

***Research Professor Brené Brown says
we are the most stressed,
depressed, overweight,
over-medicated society in history.***

Stress is handled differently by different people, because – we're all different! What stresses you? How do you handle your stress?

Whether it's a presentation you have to deliver, a job interview, your wedding, your divorce, your finances, a book you're trying to finish… the list can be endless!

When I'm facing stresses of life, I tend to procrastinate (which BTW is a manifestation of self-doubt) and I can often end up sabotaging my own success. I think we have a tendency to doubt our strengths and abilities, because we're exposed to countless messages and advertising from mainstream media that make us feel inferior and doubtful about our abilities and strengths.

Here are two questions I use to help nurture my growth and resilience:

Question #1: What Do I Fear, and What's the Worst Outcome?

Write it down! The act of writing something down has a powerful effect on our psyche. It helps give clarity to the actual reality vs what we are imagining. Chances are that your fear doesn't pose a threat to your life and wellbeing. If it does, then you definitely need to take subversive action. But, it's also important to reflect on events that stressed you in the past, and how you managed to come through unscathed and alive!

Remember: Worry and stress are the interest we pay on debts that never come due.

When you're fearing the "worst" outcome of a situation, adapt a "what if?" approach. Make a list of all the worst outcomes you can imagine for whatever scenario is stressing you out.

Now, you're ready to answer…

Question #2: What Can I Do to Succeed, and What Will I Do?

I admire what Henry Ford accomplished in his lifetime. He was brilliant! One of my favourite quotes from him is: *"Whether you think you can, or you think you can't, you're right"*.

It's a great quote, but it's also important to remember that the power of words is very powerful. Words feed our thoughts, and our thoughts feed our results.

Our competence is measured by the word "can." If you're having any doubt about your strengths and abilities, that question *"What can I do to succeed?"* might bring up feelings of hopelessness, doubt, fear, and frustration.

Conversely, the word "will" is about action! It primes you to come up with options, and assumes you have what it takes to succeed.

It's important to remind yourself of incidents in the past when you overcame challenges by using your personal strengths (and all the strategies you used). This will help move you from a mindset of "I can't" to "Damn it, YES, I can, and I will!"

Another great strategy is to act *"as if"* it's already your reality. That's a great way to overcome the internal roadblocks to success. When you pretend that everything's going great and your results are exactly what you want, it sends a message to your brain that "all is well." Your brain doesn't know the difference between reality and fantasy.

"Fake it 'til you make it" has scientific basis, because it bypasses the emotional brain. When you fake it, you convince your emotional brain that all is safe, even if the potential danger is still present. And given that the danger is rarely real, that's not a bad thing after all, right?!

Being Positive in a Negative World

While I was giving a power-of-positive-media presentation, an attendee said "It's hard to be positive, with all the negative stuff going on in the world."

Yes, it sure can be! It's helpful to remember that, in order to maintain a positive mindset, we need to **avoid the opposite mindset**.

There are lots of people and messages/images that can magnify all the reasons to be negative. We're bombarded with those messages and images through mainstream media for countless hours every day. Think of it. We spend an average of 6 hours every day staring at a media screen – whether it's your phone, your computer, your tablet, or your TV – we're exposed to some form of media for a whopping third of our lives!

I encourage everyone I meet to take *the diet that really works: a media fast. Don't watch, read, or listen to news and FEEL how much your life improves!*

I'm not suggesting that you hide under a rock and pretend that everything is perfect. Just be aware of your surroundings. When you feel like a situation or discussion is turning toward anger, resentment, envy, or hostility in any form, then you know it's time to change your environment, your thoughts, and your conversations.

When like-minded people get together, they magnify their vibrations/consciousness. Start finding ways to commune with others who want more positivity in their lives. Keep in mind that *we become the company we keep*. We are the sum total of the five people we spend the most time with.

I was reminded by Deepak Chopra that a positive mindset expands like a ripple to our relationships, our community, and ultimately the world.

So, let's get rippling!

Time For a Change?

Have you ever wanted to change a bad habit? It can be a frustrating experience, especially when it's being underlined by the countless advertising promises we see/hear every day for quick and easy solutions... for everything from weight loss, to finding your dream job or soulmate. It's no surprise that many of us begin to feel completely inadequate, and join the more than 90 percent of people who eventually give up on their goals.

Change takes work... but it's relatively easy!

If you really want to change some part of your life, there are a few simple and effective steps you can take.

Behaviours that become habits create neural pathways in our brains. These pathways are made from the mindless repetition of certain behaviours – things like brushing our teeth a certain way, dressing in a specific sequence, putting on our seatbelt – things that are done the same way every day.

The good news is that we can create new pathways by changing our behaviour. When we consistently practice "new" behaviours, we can create new neural pathways and overcome bad habits!

I like to think of it as walking a new path in a forest where no-one has gone before. If we walk that same, NEW path every day our footsteps eventually create a well-trodden trail. Then we can enjoy watching the grass grow over the path we've chosen to no longer walk.

Here are a few things you can practice to bring about change:

GET CLEAR ON WHAT YOU WANT

I love to use a practice called "Clarity/Contrast" to become crystal clear on what I want.

We're great at defining what we don't want or like in our lives, but it can be challenging to define what we actually want. That's why the Clarity/Contrast exercise is an effective way to get clear on your goals. This technique was taught to me by Michael Losier, best-selling author of *Law of Attraction: the Science of Getting More of What You Want and Less of What You Don't.*

Grab a piece of paper, draw a line down the middle, and title each column:

CONTRAST (What I don't want)	CLARITY (What I want)
Clients who keep cancelling	Clients who keep commitments
Boyfriend who cheats	Boyfriend with integrity
Smoking habit that stinks	Healthy lifestyle

Be clear on the habit/behaviour you want to change, and the new one you want to manifest in your life.

IMAGINE HOW THAT CHANGE WILL MAKE YOU FEEL

Activate your imagination to envision your future with your desired results. Keep your Clarity/Contrast list with you and refer to it daily. It's important to really feel the emotions of having your desires fulfilled. Imagine your new life with your desired results, and enjoy those feelings for as long as possible! We can often overlook the positive things that happen in our life because of the hectic pace we keep most days. But once you become aware of this tendency to fast-forward through life, the easier it becomes to stop and savour the positive moments. Savouring these moments help embed them into our subconscious mind to create new, positive neural networks that help reinforce positive emotions. So the next time you practice your positive behaviour, take a moment to let those good feelings sink in, and another to remind yourself of your power in making it happen. Making this a regular practice can go a long way in manifesting lasting positive change in your life.

BE CONSISTENT

Goals/Dreams without an action plan are mere fantasies. Consistent and persistent action toward your goals and dreams will bring results, guaranteed. That is not a fantasy; it's the reality of our universal laws. The law of attraction is an obedient force of the universe that reacts to consistent action… negative and positive! Once you start practicing positive habits (and get rid of negative ones), you will start seeing positive results. It's the LAW.

Change takes effort, but it gets easier the more you go through the process.

- Define what you want by using the Clarity/Contrast exercise
- WRITE IT DOWN and refer to it daily
- Take consistent and persistent action
- Give your desires attention, energy and focus
- Savour the feeling of your desires already fulfilled
- Celebrate your wins
- Remove doubt by looking for evidence of abundance and success
- Repeat the process
- Enjoy forging new pathways!

Learn to Love
All That You Are
and
Resign with Good Grace
All That You Are Not.

Why is it that learning to love ourselves is one of the hardest things we'll learn to do in our lifetime?!

Part of the reason is biological, I think. We humans were born with something called a "negativity bias." It's part of our biology... part of our evolution. We became hard-wired to dismiss the good things in our life, because we always needed to be on a constant lookout for danger in our midst, and threats to our life.

As we evolve into the 21st century, this bias is now fed by negative messages from advertising and mainstream media that keep telling us we're never enough: we're never smart enough, never rich enough, never attractive enough, and definitely never slim enough!

Any wonder that we grow up feeling inferior, unworthy, and doubtful about the goodness that exists within us?!

So, how do we even begin to offset this negativity that nags at us? How can we start to appreciate all the good things in the world, all the good people doing good things in the world, and all the goodness that exists within us?

How do we start to convince ourselves that we are deserving and worthy of love?

We need to replace the negative belief with a new, positive one. A belief is just a thought that we keep repeating to ourselves over and over and over again. So, we need to be the "gatekeeper" of our mind. We need to filter the messages we allow into our mind.

To start feeling loveable, we first need to start defining and appreciating our good qualities. In the hustle-bustle of life, it's often easy to dismiss the nice, simple things we do every day... things like holding a door open for someone, or letting someone go ahead of us at the grocery checkout, or leaving enough room for someone to cut ahead of us in a traffic jam.

- What if we started to define these simple gestures as expressions of kindness, decency, and goodness?
- What if we started to dismiss all the negative messages from advertising and mainstream media that keep telling us we're inferior?
- What if we kept repeating positive messages to ourselves to create a new belief that we're essentially good people and worthy of love?

In my quest to grow a Universe of Love, I created a Mindfulness Manifesto, a Triple A, 7-Day Formula to Make Peace with Stress. Included in the manifesto is an mp3 of affirmations I created for myself years ago so I could listen to positive messages every night while I fall asleep. I'd love to share it with you here:

https://gottalovelove.com/mindfulness-manifesto/

My wish for you is to always...
Live Well
Laugh Often
Love Always
Be Mindful
and
Stay Positive

DAD'S INSTRUCTIONS FOR LIFE

- *When facing a difficult task, act like it's impossible to fail.*

- *Patronize local merchants, even if it costs a bit more.*

- *Stop and listen to street musicians, and leave a donation.*

- *Learn to say no quickly & politely so you don't spread yourself too thin.*

- *Substitute the word problem with the word opportunity.*

- *Life isn't fair, so the sooner you accept that the better.*

- *Do what needs doing when it needs to be done and resist procrastinating.*

- *Praise in public, and criticize in private.*

- *Set your values and don't compromise. Nobody ever lies in their deathbed and says, "If only I'd spent more time at work."*

- *Learn to admit, "I don't know," and learn to say "I'm sorry."*

- *Live beneath your means, and pay yourself first.*

- *Treat everyone you meet the same way you want to be treated.*

- *Keep secrets, and never gossip.*

- *Instead of learning tricks of the trade, learn the trade.*

- *Admit your mistakes.*

- *Never cheat.*

- *Sit in silence often, because opportunity knocks softly.*

- *Pray for courage and wisdom instead of things.*

- *Never take action when you're angry.*

- *Never underestimate the power of forgiveness.*

- *Be punctual, and insist that others are.*

- *Have good posture and enter a room with confidence & purpose.*

- *Never pay for work before it's completed.*

- *Beware of the person who has nothing to lose.*

- *Say please & thank you a lot! Make gratitude a daily practice!*

ABOUT THE AUTHOR

Tanya MacIntyre spent 22 years being immersed in bad news every day, working as a broadcaster in mainstream media.

She packed up negative news for positive media, and founded The Good News Only in 2010 to be a resource for people to watch, read, and hear GOOD things to help you FEEL GOOD.

Tanya currently lives in Ontario, Canada with her husband of 25+ years, Lance.

Tanya hosts a weekly radio show, The Good News Only (where you only hear GOOD things to help you FEEL GOOD), and she teaches people to be their own guru by hosting regular workshops and seminars on how you can create and maintain clarity, purpose, & mindfulness in your life and make peace with your stress.

**Contact Tanya for your
Workshops, Seminars, Keynotes
to inform & inspire!**

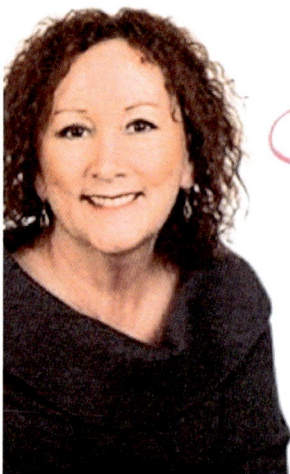